ISBN-13: 978-1-942500-08-7
ISBN-10: 1-942500-08-7

Produced by
Boulevard Books
220 Hylan Boulevard
Staten Island, NY 10305

Table of Poetics

All is Just in the Eye of the Beholder

Where Angels Reside

Middle of the Night

Kiss Me, My Love

For Valentine's Day

I would if I could

The Fate

And the Leaves Fall Down

Words for Company

Carried

So in Love

Desire

Fall Foliage

The Butterfly Dance

November

Just another Note

Fade into the Sunrise

So it Shall be

Fortune Teller

Wind Song

Love Unexpected

Walk into the Light

For You

Rage

Four seasons

Remembrance

Rain Drop

Come Springtime

In a Kiss

What is it?

Grounded to the Earth

Blood Moon

The American Dream

Autumn Moon

Cover Me

Link to Chain

Over the Rainbow

Over my Head

To Plant a Garden

Charles Town

Beauty is in the Eye of the Beholder

My Heart Flutters by

The Narcissist

Entitled

Muse

High

Turquoise

Everlasting

Daydream

I Cannot Capture the Moon

The Sound's Calling

Unrequited Love

Inspire

It's in the Little Things

Simply Mortal

Like a Pearl

My Skin is Pretty

I am Responsible

The Pine Tree

The Little Boat that could

What is the Price?

My Beloved

Until I Found You

Desire

The Entitlement of the Soul

Book I

By Palma Di Bello Mingozzi

Man Made

All my words
Let them burn
And singe blood to paper
Scattering my dust
To air and water
The scorching of my breath
 is voice to fire

I wrote a lifetime's worth
I wrote for him
and flagellated me
Chasing a lust that's
closer to my heart's appeal

I wrote to bleed
I wrote to feel

Captive of my own sweet dreams
I knew how to please
I wrote and he loved me

I wrote and he lied to me
I wrote and
freedom finally kissed me.

Spirit, the Muses and I

Spirit won't let me die
No matter how cold it is outside

Spirit won't let me down
When I stumble and cry

Between shadow and light
Spirit is strength from the eye

He comes to dine
And penetrates the mind

Spirit brings to light
All of the muses

Come to feast
At my table at night

Spirit, the Muses and I shake hands
And eat from the source of life

That we may bring
All to see the infinite sky

A drink from the cup of Zeus
All is born from the fountain of youth

We open the door
To the portal of life and death is alive

And dance through the soul
Of every star in the Universe

Spirit won't let me die
I am the infinite voice of life

Visceral masculine ardent flower
Who's Cardinal rule is masked in power.

Letting go

I stood
Outside in the frigid night
Looking up at the crescent moon

It was cold
And I felt the troubled voice
Of my own thoughts

Nothing stirred
Not even the leaf of a pine cone
Moved by its own soul

It was silence
That whispered
Upon my path

I wondered why
I should come to pass
On such a night
And light covers sight

I closed my eyes

And waited
Engulfed in a sorrow
That was made to last

I prayed for the strength
To let go of the past
That he should have
as it lives in me
The joy that entity breathes.

The Artist Alive

When my artistic Muse
Calls me from thin air
I answer right away
No work is done unawares
I slave all night and day
Without a care
Pure vision is a pixie of enchantment
The canvas a debonair endowment
The artist never quite doth sleep
The dream of feathers in flight of fancy
She loves in beauty ardently
Lit by flame and possibility
The folds of texture
The lines of time in shape and form
For a sfumato to the dark
Is shade existing by the light
The brush is to the call
The color of the soul
The sound that lulls
All to come home.

Imagine

Welcome comrades
To the corner of simplicity
Where thought is ode to intimacy
Dwelling in silence's image

A seemingly endless possibility
I implore an ear
To an enriching forte
stay elegant, you say
And the portrait is born again

For what is poetry
If not the divine intervention
Of her lover
A word and I cannot falter

Ah but I do ramble on so
I adore a voice among stars
On a cloudy night
The brilliance of which I
Can never do without

Take away the light from my eyes
Take my ears
My lips
But leave me to my heart
I will still be
The voice
That gives light to a psalm.

Love Me

How can you say you love me
When I don't even love myself

Perhaps the one thing
The only thing that has true meaning
Is the one thing that keeps on giving

But I don't know what it means to be so open
And I keep on living

In all things life is a secret
Amongst the many that are hidden
This is the script I've been given
That I don't know what love is

What it is that you want to pull out from me?

It cannot be endure and
What I placed inside its core
exists and is written upon stone
One that I have placed upon my soul

I cannot be for you
What you dream of holding
For a statue in form and posture
Is a porcelain doll
Formed in childhood

You want to give so ardently
And I don't know what to do with this

I want to believe
I really do
That somehow somewhere
There are feelings bathed
In the all-encompassing
Field of emotion
That red is the color of passion
But I have no true offering

I cannot keep you from falling
And kissing the soles of my feet
But my heart
This never ending pounding of self-glorified drumming
has cast itself
Into the shadow of its own darkness

No light can ponder it

Every fragmented piece has been folded up neatly
Into the flesh of its own deprived state of identity
It remains broken under the fading
Glimmer of passing evening-tides
I linger still under the moonlight

Thoughts singed life with indifference
I cannot be for you the rose in the desert

Two are the birds in flight
Two are the flames that expire in the night
My light has called in the white flag of surrender
Then the flint of my desire

Burnt itself out

I cannot love you, you see
I cannot love you, don't ask it of me
It's the impossible dream
You ask too much of me
Because I don't know how to be
At least it's always been this way for me
I cannot love you as you love me

And time remains unchanged
Under the siren's melody
I hear the pealing sound of laughter
Kept at a distance
The Ocean a lull of waves
A cry inside its own resistance

The clinking of champagne glasses celebrating dreams and rites of fertility
Will you marry me?
And I'm brought back to reality.

Let Me

Will you let me paint the stars
Under satiny pearls
Of comets in flight

Let me be huntress
For your hungry eyes

Will you let me call your name
In utter compassion
Renounce all of my earthly possessions

Will you let me desire
Our Universe to life
Will you let me dream
Our future as one

Will you let me
Care for you
When you're feeling down
Will you let me
Take your hand into mine
Go on a train ride before I die
Without renaming the journey only mine

Will you let me
Play with you in fields of daisies
Where we can lie still
And breathe in each other's whispers
Will you let me caress your hair
With tender care

Trade kisses in moistened lips

Will you let me hold you
In a soft embrace
And keep you tightly bound to my heart and for all time
With my body and mind
Will you let me rename the stars?

Will you let me love you
While there is still time
Say yes and I will call you still,
Always and Forever Mine.

Autumn Sun

May you always walk softly
Upon the Earth
Resting on yielding moss
And may the leaves upon the trees
Be the coverlet
To the soothing desires
Of a heart in calling
The sun is to the eye
The spirit of time
Autumn is always
Amorously divine

Désiré

My Désiré
Do you conspire against me?
Wherefore I mentioned
The intricacy of patience
Do you weave a tapestry of isolation?
Oh but the intrigue of my starvation
Is portraiture to diffident derision
Désiré
Do not turn your face away
For tears are lighter than diamonds
And the skin of your soul
Is brighter than the stars in darkness
Who can say
What He and His choir of angels
in his hierarchy profess
In the languor of your touch
The fabric of your smile
Lingers on
Of lavender and plumes
Silks and white satins
My Désiré, sweet, sweet Desire
I dream the scent of your softness
And the embodiment
of a perfume to your likeness.

Never Let Me Go

Follow the road to Freedom
Find the path in every season
Be that confident song of reason

Discover the rhythm of a canzonetta
Dance to life's Operetta

Take me with you
Into the light of wisdom
Remember the elders
Be moved by the elements

See how she trembles
The vibratory angel
Whose voice is tended to the birthing of nature
Man is the hierarchy of animals

Utter the cry of appeal
Feel how she speaks
See how she sees
Listen to the wind

Never let me go
Even the stars know
Where you belong

Sing to You

Sing to the world
A song of adoration
Let the angels trumpet out of habit
The Lord adorns with prideful scorn
The sunrise tames the rightful storm
He comes to me when I call him love
Shall I string a necklace of devotion
For I love you more than the glaciers
And all the verdant mountains
Profoundly deep, infinitely immense
My field of cultivation
The darling to entire nations
Laurels and flowers
Shall fall to your feet
And I shall guide you to my bed
And cover your skin
 with my entire body
The warmth of which will
Crimson the altar of your lips
And minister the hair upon your head
And bless the strand of red
binding you to my living breath.

Freedom

Follow the road to Freedom
Find the path in every season
Be that confident song of reason

Discover the rhythm of a canzonetta
Dance to life's Operetta

Take me with you
Into the light of wisdom
Remember the elders
Be moved by the elements

See how she trembles
The vibratory angel
Whose voice is tended to the birthing of nature
Man is the hierarchy of animals

Utter the cry of appeal
Feel how she speaks
See how she sees
Listen to the wind

Never let me go
Even the stars know
Where you belong

Anonymous

A petal wilts lying under cover
Awakened skin
The shiver of my inner power
Nestled fingers upon sweet lips
She calls the frost the dream
Of a thousand forests
I burn for you
As pure wildflower
You have awakened my desire.

All is Just in the Eye of the Beholder

Surely the voice of a poet is always loud and obnoxious and including
rude and tenacious

Surely looking down upon the stage
at a million faces that search him for meaning
he shoves his nose into the ground and sniffs like a dog the gravel of his
own excrement

Surely the voice of the poet grows larger than life in the moment of glory
Because he is not a woman
Marking her territory

Surely this makes all the difference

And Aren't we all a little bit indifferent

Surely confidence thrives in the manner of speech
And he rises beyond the stars
Lulling everyone with his outcry
At the moment in which it is received
Surely He finds himself
Throwing caution in the wind
Yes indeed he becomes subliminal weight.

And the Universe waits upon his word and living condition
Posing a problematic solution of the notion

"All that is, becomes!"

And the pendulum swings unevenly speaking of execution

Delivering a message is no easy accomplishment
I hope you are listening

He trembles as a leaf floating in the wind
in front of his periwinkle audience
Bearing the indistinguishable mask of weakness
glued to the face of his own perpendicular facet

You cannot see it as I imagined it
It takes courage
Not to be monotonous
All is synchronicity
All is harmony
The spotlight is named insanity
Covering body and form in lucidity

He speaks in truth
The trauma that is the portrait of his life
When the croaking of his sound
Is heard in the distance
The response
Is the cackling call of the rooster

He shakes and he shivers and his lips quiver in trebled confidence and his
hands fold into his feebleness
Bending his head down low
The hand caresses the sweat gathered upon his forehead
He leaves the stage giving space to the next person

But don't let me tell you
Because you wouldn't believe it
Only women tremble when speaking in public

It's a weakness in the knees
That gives birth to wings
Announcing to the extremities
The longevity of eternity

Softly and fragrantly
She is birthed in love's controversy

A lioness sees the center of her pride
Pitching her roar upon scales of time
She cannot remain silent

The intricacy of a mind is a work in progress
Intelligence is born to woman
So is creativity and higher consciousness
We are not made only of fluff and stuff
She finds in herself the power of her own mastery

But don't let me tell you any of it
Since I'm the one that left at home my precious gifts
The paper upon which all is whole
That paper of indignation
Ridiculous and so called holy
Giving rise to proclamation
And then there is only resignation

Poets speak in the aftermath of a dream
Who is he?
Who is she that cannot dream?
Who are you that cannot see beyond your own tears?

All is

All is

But I am just this
A woman rooted in justice
In the eye of the beholder
All is just
Even when vision is lost
All is just in thought and
All is simply just thought
Pure and Untouched

In the eye of the dreamer
All is life giving
The beholder is the eye of the caterpillar
The iris its wings
her fancy a reflection upon still waters
Intelligence is born within the light of a star
And we are all born of its dust.

Where Angels Reside

On the platform of life
Liberty resides
Dance, dance, dance
To the beat of the drum
For the heart beats in ecstasy
Where do Angels reside?
In the temple of glory
In the Word, in a song
In a name unrecognized
In the irony of life
IN THE FLESH?
Cry out!
For the thunderbird reigns
In the oceans fire
Ride on the wave of desire
I call him my profound
I mark him mine.

Middle of the Night

I rise with the luminous moon
Stand in the middle of the room
Gaze down upon its swollen beam
Am I still dreaming in between?
Something stirs inside the night
That something or someone
That holds my face inside a palm
The hand that so caressed
The tender flush upon my flesh
Making me quiver all over again
This night I think of you
Can't say
I don't know what to do
Because I know you feel it too
I only know
I want to be with you
As sword to stone
As pearl inside the tiny shore
I race for you
I run to you
I call your name
I long for you
And in the silence of a dormant house
For you my love
For you
I shiver right on through.

Kiss Me, My Love

Kiss me in the light of the day
Before the sun fades away
Kiss me and let my words disintegrate
Into the archway of your sweet embrace

Kiss me my love
I've waited so long
And let the breath of my soul
Sing to you a whimsical song

My bounty is yours
My body your home
Kiss me my love
And let the eye fall where it may

The groove of my neck
A mystical plain
The rise of my breast
Your ample conclave.

For Valentine's Day

I thought to make you
A large bouquet of paper red roses
With bows of silken white satin
Harpooning in my humectant perfume
I thought that even the sun
Would envy the ardor of my words in their brilliance
I have you in my sight
A vision of aromatic flavor
As mountain cover to landscape
I long to breathe your February air
Crimson is the color of my love
I thought to dedicate it all
In full ardor
In full devoted armor
For the glint of my sword
Bleeds with a passion
That only your thirst can conquer
So I fashioned this poem
To sing you my song
No greater love exists in the world
Than a deep heart in devotion
I love the core of your profound emotion
You are my strength
Our love is a petal trembling in weakness
Devouring dew upon skin
I see you from within
I love, love, love you
My prince.

I Would if I Could

I would,
I would
If I could
I would if I could
Sing to you all
But I don't have a voice
So I won't
I would if I could
Fix my crooked teeth
If I could I would
But I don't have the money
So I don't
I could
I really think I could
Change the world
If I could I would
But I can't
So I don't

I leave it alone.

The Fate

She quivers as the new day in the sun
Happiness is a song now undone
As the stone turns to gold
She is risen alone
Showered in morning glory
The raindrop and the dew
Are the residue of the leaf
Resting on its grass blade
She is holding the stalk of wheat
Emanating her conceit
Flowers are crowned from her bosom
The strand of her conviction
Life is her chariot in color textured wind
Every mirror shatters at the sound of a brick
Break the glass and the sand will fire it
See her for her sandaled feet covering
She is the walk of the moonlight
Gathering the seed in twilight
Seated at the ridge of the mountain
She is the roar of the lioness
Conqueror of fate and direction
Fare for a compass on the dark voyage at night
Tis the star that appears in the dark
And the morning is become aware
Of the shift in the light
Her spear tossed into the sky.

And the Leaves Fall down

I think it's beautiful when so many leaves fall from the trees, all that ochre and crimson spread out before the pavement, adorning the grass that contains it. Those perfect little droplets inside the color spectrum of the rainbow before our eyes.

As far and wide as the eye can see, the streets are fat and heavy. I think they are these brilliant gems
that sense the coming of change in the air.

As the sun fills it with brilliance there is no gap between the color that permeates everywhere
and into the nothing.

Yellow to orange, red, and gold and always to golden brown, it's all around delight. I think it's great to follow the path, crunch a few leaves under out feet and call the day ever so sweet. Today I feel complete, sensing a crisp scent of woodland in the vicinity.

I follow the mastery of deep rooted proximity and walk alongside of creation, nurturing the mystery, the passion of true and ever present evanescent nature.

Words for Company

Inside this old house
you'll find no bricks
scattered about
only the rigidly bound
De-Veining of a poet's
Roe and verses.
Lying still inside the bookshelves
of faded pages
Yellowed with
Marauding existence
In what is to be believed
Of its own accord
Reality and the surreal occurring.
Meeting side by side
In an encyclopedia of
Words for company
That which is the lyrical component
Of the existential is the
Song of the survivor.
The violin player plunders on
and the accompaniment applauds
Upon the awakening
of a solitary dreamer
Resting his head
on the shell of his idle skull.

Carried

I compare you to the Verdi's symphony
In Winter's daydream
the sweetest harmony
in uncharted melody.
I have only just taught her today
she's got your name on it
your soul exists in it.
She's got that longing to be heard
Traveling and crossing every boundary
inspiring a song in me.
Transport the sound of love
it's my infinite voice
that longs to be heard
for you are mine alone to hold.
Never was there a sweeter hope
than one found on this road.
This journey,
a collision of musical reverie
She speaks to me ever so peacefully.
Longingly,
And breathing new life into me
She gives birth to all my felicity.
She bears all things in need
Can I bring this joy to you
Dare I to dream in loveliness?
The song
She carries me
Indeed she carries me
To your wings.

So in Love

Dripping with ardor
So in love with fervent desire
Voices call to a harbor
Even the cavern mourns unexplored in the forest

He murmurs in wishes
She bears silken caresses
and passions become declarations
What is the sum of all parts of a cajoled kiss?

But oh my darling,
Listen to my words
How can I be anything other
Than a woman of force?
In love with your fire
Welded into your arms
As metal born to flame
The sword is to the stone
The melatonin of skin
I am alive, soft and hard
Always devoted and ever so kind
Adoring wide open spaces
Softening to wider expanses
Lips to pearly gleams of protruding white teeth
Captured in a kiss

Blame it on my beautiful hips
And wind blowing on mountain peaks
Is there anything more beautiful?
Than an umbilical dream
The body is a highway

And belly is unearthed
through the soul of my hands
Venus reigns
Living the life of a harlot
For your eyes only
How can I be anything other
Than Perfect?
Dripping with ardor
So in love with fervent desire
You are and will always be flame to my fire.

Desire

Because my soul craved
Then here is my love
All knowing
Thought in emotion
My heart beating
in complete devotion

Because my soul craved
Here is the nature
Of my true form
I color it whole
On the wings of a dove

Here is my life
Take only what you can hold

My feelings unchanged
Desiring
For he was that side of me
Covenant of ecstasy

Because my soul craved yours
I fly above as below, once more.

Fall Foliage

I'm overwhelmed
By the falling leaf
Pirouetting before me

I'm overwhelmed
by the naked beauty
Standing before me

I will have no Joy
Until the Tree
Becomes full foliage

I will have only this image
That which moves from within
Between dream and reality

I will have no Peace
Until I lose myself profoundly
Grounded into the heap.

The Butterfly Dance

Tossed along from desert to wind
She dances to ancient beat.
When you see her
Recognition is clear.
The mystical vision of
glory and determination
Inclining her to the perfume
Inside the sacred feminine.
She is perpetual motion
She is the all inspiring womb of devotion.

She mesmerizes and shakes up
The memory of her ancestry
Her wings a tremble of joy
Inside the air she is gathering and
Gliding in ode and soaring
To the Heavens above
She to the stars is the rendering of the whole.

Her hair a bliss of recovery
Her smile a gleaming dose of reality
She is
The knowledge of fairies in every wood covering.
How shall I describe her ordinary?
She is the Sun and the Moon in Aries
Her eyes the gleam of prosperity.
She is the arch in the scent of all rainbows
The smell of rain drops in autumn crescendo.

Gathering leaves in motion
She moves the wind with devotion.
Her spirit takes leave
Flapping her wings over nature and emotion.
She opens the magical portal

Belonging to all and nothing.
In her is appeal
that which attracts us all
to the absolute cosmic everything.

She is voice to the base of humanity
The rhythm of bones and remains.
In all her flight and agility
A woman of honor
Sincerity and ardor.
She is the color
Of greatness and armor.
She dances for you and for me
She dances for her own beauty.

She dances for she is destiny
The memory of ardent dreams.

She dances and opens her wings
She dances pure form and bliss.

And she dances for she is free
And blows into you another dream.

She dances upon your soul
and she remains within.

November

Nothing,
No winter storm
As cold
As the fold
Of snowflake
Falling upon my face
Feels quite as cold
As hail and wind
In treacherous rain
November storms in as a snare
The snake of all bewares
Stealing my sight unaware
Shattering the heart
As pieces of glass
Mirroring my solace and regret
Where is my coat?
The vain part of my love
Has cast it upon the miserable shore
and the rain is tear to
My cursed and confounded blood.

Claudette

Beautiful proses
Like all the roses
Bent over the ocean
Calling the wave a recluse emotion
Who came to see her causes?
Flushed under peculiarity
The treble of conviction
Makes for such a commotion
The ship collides with the vision
A journey is only a marker for an unruly condition
Ink is to penmanship
That which fades on paper
She is the loom
Of her own configuration
Of what use is calligraphy
If not the Ode of illicit dreams

The scream of the hunt
The plight of the lions roar
And the prey is taken up whole
Adored in a poetic verse
That which could not be conversed
And the pages turn
The lyric will burn
As for a sonnet
The writer kept her under close scrutiny
His pages covert
His thoughts locked in a drawer called torment.

I am She

I am she
Haggard witch rising
Out of the swamp marshes
Spume of the sea
Deity of beauty

I am she
Frailty of spirit
Delicate petal of roses
Wind, Rain, Sun and Proses
Cluster of stars
Guiding sea faring mermaids

I am she
Tears of the Muses
Game for the masses
I am all that is bound
I am the mother and her nucleus
I am that which is
And has always been
The nature of woman
Human and man's nutrient.

Never Let me Go

Cover me
With the freshness
Of Ocean waters
Drowned under
The wave of ecstasy
I know only this

Cover me
With the breath of life
Sealed with a kiss
To paradise
And Oh do not be so far removed
That I can no longer see through you

For I will find you
As you have followed
I will always have you
For in this life
My womb sings
In you I find
The elixir of my release

Never let me go
And the Muses dance
And Venus speaks
Do not be afraid
Of Death's Kiss.

Sweet Dreams my Love

Sweet dreams my love
I've been to New York
Thought I'd find you
Some trinket designed
With the fire of my love
But bless your heart
What I thought was nice
Was simply a man
Sitting down holding a
Papillion and whistling a tune
Carving on paper the name

Of his wound
Folded up in song
He sang and was lost
I came to New York
To buy you a dove
A symbol of my love
But bless my soul
I found only a pigeon
Perched on a bench
Waiting for the man
To feed him his crumbs
Upon the cement.

Where are the Roses?

Where are the roses
When the sun goes down
And the curtain closes

Where are the roses
When life comes calling
Silently crawling

Where are the roses
When the colt's gallop whines
Clinks and clanks of insanity

Where are the roses
When the princes have notions
Uninhibited by the oceans

Where are the roses
When conceived in familiar poses
Beckon unmoved by children's voices

Where are the roses
At their final stages
Dressed in familial self atrocity

Where are the roses
Lethargic in tumultuous waters
Accepting the abhorrence of violence

Where are the roses
Crawling with petals of silence

Questioning the call of patience

Where are the roses
The fragrance of her proses

The Act of Freedom's Boredom

Where are the roses
In the hour of destruction
A phrase or a farce in the will of consumption

Where are the roses
Reaping and raping in a crimson vocation
Held at the helm of victimization.

One Seed

One seed cannot
Make for a forest breathe
One seed cannot change
The world You see
One seed is a Catastrophe
Yet
In multitudes
The pines and the oaks
The cherry woods and the chestnuts
The Maples and the redwoods
Spread out across the land
Giving us a sense of belonging
One seed cannot make the forest
But the Earth blossoms
Our home is modest
One seed and she ripens
One seed and she opens
One seed and she enlivens
Enriching with ancestry
Endowing with messages
One seed
Caressing our senses
Entertaining our eyes
Spectacular in divinity
One seed and we are plunged in beauty.

Pipe Dreams

They keep telling me they are pipe dreams
Who came up with this terminology
It's time to come to terms with the salesman's death
We cannot live in the resurrection of the past
They keep telling me they are pipe dreams
Pipes bring water to the cities
Rejuvenating life amongst the living

We are fire stars and drops of water

I have an intentional ardor
Whose name burns bright
No lesser than the stars

In the grand aqueduct of life
I am that which I am
A dreamer
Alive.

Silence

I don't want this silence
I want utter chaos
that follows me everywhere

I don't want to sit in silence
Like a child sitting in a corner
Looking at the White washed spaces

I don't want to think about silence
It's a punishment and a sacrifice

I don't want to be silent
Not much has ever been accomplished
Sitting alone in the darkness

They call it quiet contemplation
For me it is a torture chamber

Awaken the Frankenstein
The need to come alive
Is not found in the walls
Of a fine brick House

Being alone
Being alone, being alone
Is madness
I don't want to find it

I don't want to pray in silence
Contemplating divine absolution

I don't want to
I don't want to be still
I just want to be Me
Enjoying myself in your company.

Remorse

I don't know why
You did this
From the beginning
I don't know what you were thinking

I don't know why I did this
I don't know what I was thinking
From the beginning
I was trembling

Like a leaf in her prairie
A butterfly blooming
A flower budding in the dark

You made me happy, I was alive

I pleaded you conceded
I could not leave it
I could not bear it
I could not escape it

I don't know why I was so senseless
I only know that when
Cupid's arrow struck me
I felt that I had died
And gone to Heaven

And now that Heaven
died before my eyes
I cannot dry the tears

You left behind

I cannot hide the pain
Behind my smile

In the pursuit of excellence
I do not want a road to nothingness
I do not want to walk in the path of insignificant existence

I Cannot Make You See

I cannot make you see
The forest for the trees

Nor feel
The wind caress your face

Nor taste the color of rain
I cannot place it in your hand

I cannot send music to your ears
I cannot sing a lovely phrase

I cannot have you dream
With eyes wide open
If you cannot find the horizon

I cannot make you see a golden meadow in the desert
Neither the sky covering the mantle of the Universe

I cannot touch your heart
If you do not want to love

I cannot be as you are...
A Realist, that's what you swear to call it

I may be weird
And with disdain you
Label my condition

I cannot make you see

with the eyes of a dreamer

That which is borne of me
In its entirety

I cannot even make you understand this poem
If you do not recognize it as your own.

The Blush of my Youth

I considered looking back
Though imprinted on my mind
Are the pillars of sand.

For what is youth
But a fair assessment
Of divine contribution
The aim of its perusal
Is a bit of a constant nuisance.

Ah, the chase and its pleasures
Though beauty then does fade away
Inside its conglomerate years.

Was it only today that
I looked at my wrinkles
Without hoping for a miracle.

With age comes wisdom
Yet I sought another form of comfort.

You were the apple in my eye
When I was young
You were the light in my world
When I was young.

I fell in love once
Making my contribution
I fell in love twice
I fell many times.

From a Distance

Each time
I blossomed a flower in full bloom
Every time
I felt myself
Returning with innocent laughter.

I became aware that beauty
Remains filled with passion
In the eyes of one seeking attention.

It was then that I found myself
Utterly amazed and In a daze
Relieving the blush of my youth
In the days of my altered existence
The flower
still stands
even from a distance.

The Usual Culprits

So you want to latch
onto my breast
A child at rest
Ride the wave
Reach the conclave

Borrow my wings
Break me in
But the Pegasus
Lives in the stars
And I am much too old
for that kind of dreaming
For you, I keep on giving

To fly alongside your spirited soul
Young buck in a field of thorns
Sing the song of ancients told
The breast that nourishes
Marks its territory cold
You are much too young to know

Hope is for the fairies
Concocted in their own glory
Flora and fauna
Living in a world all of their own
Apart from the eyes
That shelter a storm
The Ocean separates the Earth
And the fire continues to burn
In the loins of our fathers

In the Breath of our mothers

Hold now forever your thoughts
For knowledge is defiance
A penitent burden
For the countenance of wills
A chain of despondent diplomacy
Rule over your own entity
For we can never be
Anything other than this
The present moment
Love inside a farfetched
virtual dream
You are a delicacy
Delightful creature in the land and sea
You are much too lovely for me
A deep deep temptation you see.

My Own

Selfless
Abandon
Wrapped
In the cocoon
Of your arms
Naked breast
Against the warmth
Of your chest
Hand to soft thigh
Stroking up and down
Mound to mountain
Ardently
Conquering
Shhh darling
Don't say anything
Just hold me
Instinctively
You are mine

Just another Note

Something had me running for the hills, once, just once, though I can't remember now what it was. I was happy, so very happy, I have always been happy. I hadn't thought about anyone else but what was mine. Something had me running for the hills, once, just this one time, I thought myself in love, though now I can't remember why I cried like a broken dove. There was a longing in that top of the hill, for someone to whisper my name, to hold my hand, oh and yes, for someone to make me laugh. It was more than I could hold, this heart full of so much joy, now I can't put my finger on it, but I thought I could own it, I really did, and I never did see it coming. Couldn't understand why I could no longer breathe, as if something tugged at my soul and wrenched it out of my body, and I shook like a leaf torn from her socket, all of a sudden I had nothing. All of a sudden all that I had,all I had to offer, all that I was, meant nothing. The hills they were calling, I remember I was running, with the air for wings and I was nearly flying, I kept on moving, it was only when I stopped to think about it that he refused it, he refused it, then and only then I fell down unconscious.

Fade into the Sunrise

Ever so gently;
My mind does go wandering...

Why then,
Go ever so blindly
Into the sunrise
That is the all consuming
perjury of wills
Ardently she sits still
Fading away
Fading away

As the soul is bound to its flight
Into the distance
Seeking solace
Perhaps the sound of stillness
Calls to every person

I've been listening
There is an echo in life's breathing
A reverberating sway of trees
Always caressing the eye
Always stroking the eardrum
Always permeating the nostril
Always the taste of iodine

And the fragmented piece of gentle glass
Reflects a fragile mind
Aye but the trees these move gently back and forth
As the waves pull and regress

Calling us all home

Searching with an Eagle's view
The summit's crescendo
Looks to find the answer
The sweetest purpose
This in having learned a lesson

To have walked a passage
In Nature's repertoire
Devouring the sound of creation
And the insects and birds hold the melodies of molded devotion

And Nature binds in a cocoon of wills
The battle between tornado and lagoon

To what do I owe
The tinkling of grass blades
Tickling my feet
And the tiny space I take upon the Earth
To what do I owe this contemplative journey

And the wind takes the breath from me
And the tiny rustle of shrubs soothe my reverie
I forget that I bleed

The wind blows the colors
blindingly from me ever so gently
Solemnly I drop my gaze
I fade away
I fly away
Immersed into the sunrise.

So it Shall Be

Ah my love,
I speak to you in verse
The only language I've known
Since the beginning of time was born
Should I have been more coarse
As fine as the salt of the Earth
I would speak with you once more of love
For mine you are to hold
To dream of you
Is to transport a lover
To the Universe's cellar
Of stellar completion
You are my super nova condition
Why then do you not come to me
When I call upon your soul
Why must the muse
Beside sit once more still
And sell her laughter short
in a compass of hope
Oh dream come to me
call me once more
Just to hear his voice
She listens in silent in dread stricken gloom
In a reflecting pool
He is inside her womb
Be then the one
Pegasus to Unicorn
Awaiting her due
She sits by the pale eclipse of the moon
Awaiting her groom

Waiting to divide and conquer
And so it shall be
Her beginning and end
for an exchange
of his new entire world.

Fortune Teller

Let me not linger
In the arms of despair
Should I trip over my own two feet
With shoelaces bare
Let me fall without a care.

Altruistic mysticism
Meets linguistic cynicism
a prison of primitive symbolism
Become the prism of circumvent
With money comes renewed respect
Then shall love behave in retrospect.

The fortune teller speaks
Beware the fallen angel in your sleep
Knowledge binds in debt
The more you have, the more you want
Man made avarice his vice
Opportunity, regret his life.

Wind Song

I hear your wind song
Calling my name
Whispering
Pulling me home.

I hear your wind song
From far and wide
A falcon's flight
Reaching new heights.

I hear your wind song
Soft and new
Covering me with dark melodies
Lulling a sweet recovery.

I hear you sing
I hear you sing
Alluring sweet enchantment
Binding me with chains of ecstasy.

I hear your wind song
Fly above a tyrannical sea of words
Dark ink written upon white sheets
Open the armor within my breast.

I hear your wind song
It's all that I have left
That and all of my dreams
It's all Own and all I have to give

For fly indeed you must
But take me with you out of lust
A melody never does turn to rust
A winged falcon is never lost.

Love Unexpected

Love comes,
When you least expect it.

It is the flight of feathers
The butterflies in your stomach.

Love equals no other
It renders you fragile.

Love conquers all fears
It brings no such thing as tears.

Love comes when you are certain
Free of possession.

Love is a certainty of connection
It is the thing of hope and relation.

Love brings joy in every equation
Love is rejuvenation.

In the heart of all time
It will make you smile.

To love is never in vain
Love never dies and suffers no pain.

To love is to give all that you've got
Even when you are far apart.

When the spring mounts
The valleys and seas
All the flowers and trees
Blossom in feasts.

This inclination of melodic sensation
Renders the soul awakened.

Reminded by Nature's call
The song of the wild calls love home
We will finally know the stirring of our soul.

Walk into the Light

I'd like to taste the blood of Socrates
For I'm not so sure he bled like any other human being

Sappho there was a poetess to be
Revered she said something in the likes of this, she said,
"someone will remember us
I say
even in another time"

Oh from afar it's easy to get caught up
In simple nonchalance
It's easy to get lost in theory
And philologists.

Marcus Aurelius said,
"Dwell on the beauty of life. Watch the stars, and see yourself running
with them."
Though I don't know much about Life
I can always appreciate how the stars
Make me feel at night
And my smile is worthwhile.

Ask me why I adore John Keats
I will tell You
All beauty prevails in one single Kiss
"A thing of beauty is a joy forever"
I believe he had it right on the money.

Beauty is that timeless piece
That Poet imagine airs

It's a good day to spread our wings
Lose ourselves in the butterfly of things.

Then Socrates come along with
"The only true wisdom is in knowing you know nothing"
Once more I believe
Indeed he then like the rest of us
No semi God
No chariot to call home.

But beauty, life, wisdom and love
Together make a perfect map
For this chartered course
The day philosophy was called
The walk of life

I took a walk, I took a look
And got lost
In the deep deep thought
Called the light in my eyes
And I walked right inside
The core of it.

For You

I don't want to meet you in eternity;
I want to be your eternal.

I don't want the water to quench the fire;
I want the flame to burn all the more brighter.

I don't want to go any much further;
I want to fasten the seat belt and burn rubber.

I don't want to ride the roller coaster;
I want wings to span out of proportion.

I don't want to settle for today;
When tomorrow is taken away.

I don't want to ever be unaware;
But become your breath of fresh air.

I don't want to breathe in despair
I want to belong to your same air.

I don't want to leave when you're not there;
I wish I could walk in the woods with you somewhere.

I don't want to walk on thin ice;
I want to be the acrobat in your life.

I don't want to be your heiress;
I want to lavish you in finesse.

I don't want to be possession;
I want to become your obsession.

I don't want to give you every moment in kindness;
I want to be your super highway.

For you my gentle man are a true transparent;
It doesn't take a genius.

With all my ardent attention,
putting aside my transgressions
I would love you always with all my virtues and all my fervent kisses.

Yours forever, poetess.

Rage

I just don't know
What's in a day
My soul is running ramped today
I really want to break something
I feel a torment ahead of my tempestuous moment
don't know where to put myself
This agitation leads way to a tumultuous frustration
What's in a day
A cursing of demoralization
I yell out what about this contemplation
I cannot serve under this condition
In too much agitation
Under my skin
That's where it lives
This unending torment
Of thought in commotion
Confusion
Renders me useless
Rage greater than any great massive boulder
Explodes in a
Grandiose finale
You do not accept me
You do not accept me and
You hurt my feelings.

Four Seasons

Fall fuels anger
That Winter breaks in nature.
Spring brings Love
That Summer doth forgive.
Who can say
What will be
Between
A pair of sheets?
Perhaps the Fall
Know You me by name...
Winter knows who lives in a forget-me-not
That opportune Spring
The scent of clean air wafting
Remembrance
Still In Summer dream
Surrendering
I wish by the light of the Moon
A fair pale face reflected.

Remembrance

Let me not become forgotten
At the mercy
Of the wind blowing
I lay my thoughts
Down by the azure ocean
Whose waves palpitate
In slow moving circles
Oh if only I could be wind
Soft caressing embalming
If only I could be the bird
The one that soars so high
Then rests her head
In a nest of clouds
Oh but to fly
Into the wings of a love song
Into the arms of my love
To carry my words
Satire lyric of my soul
If only I were to be loved
How beautiful the world becomes
Into the arms of my mother
I'd suckle at her breast
The nurturing of milk and honey
Of my true divine nature
Into the depth of the Earth
I throw my body
Only to dwell, rebel and
To be reborn again.

Rain Drop

The entire world is contained
In a tiny droplet of water.

She does not fall far
From the arbor that holds her.

Upon closer inspection
She bears the name of her own reflection.

Of felicity,
So still is her conditioning.

Quiet then slowly strengthening
Gleaming brilliantly.

Shhh, I am listening
Seeking, contemplating, rejuvenating.

She makes me so happy
This little rain drop
Looking back at me.

Come Springtime

And the Birds come in revolution
Like little tiny soldiers in millions
Gathering iodine from the Ocean
Causing a great commotion
I am awakened from a deep slumber

Their sharp cries
Inundate the World
Announcing the arrival
Of springtime on Earth
The grass a shelter of their birth

Who will house such a voice?
Wings, bodies and claws
But the arbor awaits
Looks upon man
Declares I still stand

The birds come in
Like great soldiers of war
Taking a stance
Taking up space
Taking over and swallowing up the place.

We have no chance
But to accept awake
Though it may take a week
to see a bud sprout
From its deep rooted seed

The birds come first in their democratic policy.

In a Kiss

That Kiss,
Aware of
our destiny
That Kiss,
Welded
Two souls into
One single breath
Then
Dispersed into thin Air
That Kiss
Held
The essence
Of a once upon a time

My words for you
Live as you do

Sometimes
The measure of
Time, weighs

In that moment
You waste the light at night
lost In atmosphere
In the word-aphorism
The state of its own accord

Dream the

kiss is bliss.

What is it?

Everything that lives, dies
Everything that dies, lives
When young, you want to die
When old, to live
Yes, I am simply become a memory
Perhaps, I didn't explain all that I am feeling
Though It did seem to me
Something of great importance
To read is to live
To read is to dream
Imagining, without perishing inside
To ravel and fly far and wide
To Inspire!
Yet you do not hear me anymore
Every drop of ink is sealed in emotion
Every page sensation
I knew not how to lose you
I knew not how to keep you
I still have some breath left
For those colored thoughts
Though small
They are Ode to my tears
To Read so that
I may fall in love
It is in thought
That You die a little
And also live a little
Perhaps the wind unites
My words to your dreams
Perhaps you'll remember
my voice one day
And I your words
You've put me to the cross
Forgive me my Lord
I would have preferred skipping this lesson

I would have enjoyed growing up without determination
Without love you can live
Without love you can also die
Why suffer?
I would have preferred not saying
I loved
I really loved
I was alive an Eagle to her shore
I am unworthy
Of This subliminal intelligence
Of this sustaining divinity
Which keeps me bound to paper
I died many times
I died each and every time
And every time I was lost
By this eternal desire
Happy to be born
And reborn Inside your mystery
To Read is to contemplate love
To Read is a narrative shouting of tenderness
To Read is to be filled with Light and awareness
meditation and reflection
To Read brings satisfaction
If to live is to die
I would not have said
The words
 I love you
I'm at my end,
At last, I am empty and think to myself...forget
Arriving at the conclusion of my ever present realization
That I have blasphemed
That I have cursed you to Hell
That I have exalted you to the Heavens
In the presence of the Angels
Then to heck with it all
The subliminal wind
And all it recalls

I will either abhor or
I will simply adore.

Grounded to the Earth

I never could
See the stars through
A telescope
You tell me
That billions and billions
Of stars shine in the dark
That there must be billions and billions of galaxies
Do they lose their brilliance
In the day?
for it's as if they've gone away
I never could see the stars
Through a camera lens
Very few pictures
Capture the night at its best
I can only see as far as my eyes
Can take me
Those seven that do twinkle
Remain Symmetrical
And the Moon keeps them company
I was never one for telepathy
But I believe I could imagine
Thought in travesty
You can never know what's in the air
Until all your senses become aware
I think I know the night as well as anyone
I think our light is the brilliance of Universe
I think we are the stars that illuminate
I think we shine from afar
In this ground called Earth

And out there in the cosmos
We are the beacon of lighted meteors.

Blood Moon

The shadow of the sun is bathed in darkness

The shadow of the moon is bathed in light

Why does the cricket quiver
Awakening the Night

Tick Tock
Soon it will be
Red October

And the time keepers
Harvest the ashes

And the light weavers
Assemble the markers

The trumpeters keep playing to the tune of
Pink skies collapsing
And Constellations amassing

It is day, It is night
It is night, it is day

And the sun and the moon
Are the covers of distant lovers

Grounded to the Earth
The cricket's chirp is old and new
The cricket's song is heard in silence

one battle cry at a time
So loud, so loud

Inside the house the people ran.

Tehran

The American Dream

The Sky fell to the ground
Millions and millions of stars
Landed at JFK Airport
September 1979
That's how I remember it
It was night when we landed
And the lights were dancing
Before my eyes
I heard it said,
"The streets are paved in gold in America"
"You can find money in every corner"
What did I know, I was eleven years old
Jimmy Carter was President
He chose us from five other families
At least that's what my father told us
The ground seemed to burn
Before my eyes
This made me think of
The sun singeing the cement
With all the squares now making sense
Heaven transformed itself that night
Everyone that arrived saw
Their name in lights
Luxembourg was a dot on the map
Brussels was a croissant memory
I never looked back
Until I started wondering.

The door to the Sky

Let your hair
Fall where it may
And lose yourself in sentiment
If clouds caress your shoulders
They are simply words breathing
Upon the chills of your warmed skin

Every dream of the soul
Makes space in air
Remember that angels do not cry
But listen to the pain of the world

If you call to them
With an open and sincere heart
Be comforted
Because it is in the Archaic Chorus
That we travel further along.

Dreams never die
And the sweet voice of inspiration
Always responds in a thousand words
Of comforted emotion.

Autumn Moon

Slowly she comes out at night
Piercing the Sky
From Behind her cloud
Protruding from darkness
She penetrates in-luminous light

Oh Crescent Moon
Dear to me in effervescent body
All Hallows Eve approaches
Convinced and full of conviction

How shall There be a rendering
Of wholeness this night?

You hold far and wide
Holy The mystery
Of lovers delight
And covet the right
To become entwined

Always the eyes
And the heart speak of
The tale of the maiden
Begging a fervent favor

Upon
The night of the solstice
Two souls bathed in light
conjoined from a distance
Telling their heart's delight

How many dollars strewn
In silvery wishes
How many witches
Cast spells in crystal clear waters

Do sirens let fall
Naked upon the Earth
Their treasured possessions?

All Hallows Eve

Wading in waters
Droplets a-gleaming
Under the weight of silken caresses

all Hollows Eve quickly approaches
This night there will be trickery
This time there'll be no mercy

Will you be colored in scarlet
As bricks broadening
inside a Rose Garden?

The glint of a sheathe
Will the blade of her warrior
be ever so cold in winter?

Gift her a pearl
Gift her the rain
Give her a handkerchief
to pardon her tears

Give her no more and no less
than the home of her youth
For she returns alone and aloof

Autumn calls
every road a-winding
ripening In foliage its Harvest
The moon advances
The Cornucopia abundant

Eclipsing the heart
She calls the shadow of her ghost
 at the witching hour
Stroking the fires
She begs earnestly
In yearning and simple desire
To let fall love ardently
all who admire her.

Cover Me

Cover me
With a coverlet
Of roses
Oh my sweet muses
Harps and music
Do not compare
To your divinity
It is in beauty
That I Cherish
To languish in your sweet embraces
To know the memory
Of the ancients

My sweet enchanted dove
Hold me
Hold my soul
From within
In you
I am become
The song established
Sing
Sing louder
Than the waves in the ocean
The tides in silence
Come forward
Commanding in proses
Shower me in roses
In the deep deep fiery sequences
I will drink from your everlasting sources
Become drunken in your love potions
Sweet, sweet muses

Shower me in poppies
And fields of harpies
I will be the spring to your
morning glories
And play the instrument
Of my everlasting love
On the chords
Of my beating heart.

Link to Chain

I promise
That I will always love You

I promise to tell You
I love You every day

I promise to thank You
Each and every Morning

For the love You Give to me
Is beautiful

I promise never to leave You
I promise to protect You

Cherish and hold You
In light and in shadow

To always Walk beside You
Hold and never let go
Of my Hands
I promise to Sustain You
All the days of my Life

Come Rain or Shine
I promise You the stars

I will never abandon You
I promise to lose myself
Inside Your skin, mind, body, soul and all energy

My heart is yours
As yours is mine
Link to link
I promise to build with petals
A chain of melodies for
All the I love You I let fly in the meadow

I promise to live and die
With You always by my side
I promise my love
I promise You my heart
Be mine.

Over the Rainbow

A garland of flowers
Upon my head
Over and under and all around
Joyful play is heard
And so astounds

In circle of hands
Aboard the round rain-bow
We clasp the horse around the merry go round

Pretty girl be blessed In light
Be blessed In love
Transcendent in flight
Illuminated swan

Oh little princess
Walk proudly on the Earth
That You may feel The petals rising
From a lovers kiss

A mantle of violets
Upon your skin
In your nakedness
You are complete
Ready to shine
And bow down before your prize

Come together

One and all
Celebrate the marriage vow
The Queen and the King
Welcome the prince

Born to the world is an angel of hope
Born is the skin of the Earth
Joy and Felicity To one and to all
Pink ribbons, blue shoelaces
This day reigns in amazement
Felicity and joy is
Inside the leisure of the sun's burning kiss

Over my Head

Sometimes
I do not know
If it is the large Butterfly
Or the grand leaf that rests
On The breath of the Wind
I need to see
The thought
That which settles
On the fate
Of my written words
Landing on a sheet of paper
As rest comes upon its destiny
Memory transforms itself
Into small glories
The caress
Of the wind in Flight
Lives In the air
There is only
Breath
And I always
Smile
As I Escape from the mind
Looking up
In the azure sky.

All my Life
I've spent with people
Who gave themselves
Self importance
Still I listened

Since their beliefs
Were ingrained into me
I did not know any other way of being
Never questioned reality or dream
I learned over the course
Of many years
To walk away
For what is important
Is an ideal resolve
To heal oneself
Of wounds that bound
All that remains is no longer
Reason to remain in the same place
Or Reason to escape
A life change
It sounds huge
It sounds impossible
It sounds like a blow horn
I found my way in my own way
And the road which I walk
Is ever made easy
By one breath
On the path of truth and love..

To Plant a Garden

Pickin' up Lilly from the show
I ask "How did it all go?"
Pickin' up Violet up at school
Wonderin' "How you doin' too?"

They say it's all good
How about you?
How in the world are YOU?

Pickin' up Gaby
Sweet and true
Hi Baby"How's your first day in High School?

Pickin' up Franny,
She's so elementary
Always waving "see you later"
to the lunch lady
and her kindred spirit Maggie round the corner

How come? she says
You seem so sad today; can I turn a joke and make you happy?
Can I turn a poppy into a prairie?

The twinkle in her eye always makes me smile
With Gabby by her side
She will always be alright

I think they're clever
I think they shine like two bright stars
Those four brilliant eyes

Call on me expecting an ultimate answer

Franny, She always asks a lot of questions
And Gabby she's always intently listening

I tell them this is how I feel...

Some things we forget in school
Like the Past, Math, and Geography

And some we leave to the open wind
Like dreams, the future and destiny

But now my loves
You are the flowers inside my garden
And with these I shall make you a great quilt with patches
To lay upon your heads
And place yourselves to rest

So sleep, lulled by the laughter of a fairy maiden
Who'll sprinkle dust upon you haven
The beauty of my love
Will shelter you from any storm
And from inside the ground
The seed will grow
And bring you to your life
This little spot on Earth is yours and mine
And I will always carry you home
With all my might

But please,
Don't leave your dreams

Behind a desk
After the bell does ring
Always hold tight my hand
For the lifting you up means never resisting
When wings call to their duty
And letting go that's the doozy
And the path that one is quite tricky
And certainly anyone will tell you
It is never ever ever so easy.

Charles Town

Nor bench for
The Commoner

Nor smile
For the foreigner

Forgive me In begging favor
Lend me your ear and fervor

For she awaits in pleasure
Truth is a treasure of future endeavor

To all persons
The gift of righteousness

Let us Indulge the senses
With a peripheral view of the planet

Chasing rainbows over the ocean
What glory of freedom and belonging

The horses turd ascertain an impression
Thus welcomes the imprinted
Holy city of pleasure

I smell
The scent of money

It lingers in the air
Still bloodied

Blue blood
is young and never gets' old nor sold

What is the valor of flesh lost
In labor and captivity

I heard the hooves of horses
No better off today than the
Martyrs of yesterday
The cobblestones are made for walking
Come forward the ghosts of dead men haunting

Teatime and portraiture
Lend voices to walls written in betrayal

In silent remains does the patriot speak
All is well in the lord's keep

The Angel Oak calling out
To the Cypress "wade in the water"

That which held in a crescent moon
Is now a basket held in a hand of Palm with empty pockets.

Regardez votre drôit

Beauty is in the Eye of the Beholder

I liked You
I told You I loved You
I liked and I loved You
Not for the reasons
You may have thought
I loved you because
You were poor

Late in the evening
You told me your story
You were so happy
With so little in wanting
Indeed you had close to nothing

I could not buy your integrity
Could not correct your disability
Nor bleed out your infirmity

I liked and I loved you
Because you were no one
And did not ask for anything
Except to dream another dream
And you were filled with felicity

I saw you and called you my flower
My lover
My heart's desire
I loved you with all of my fire
My prince
My ardent admirer

I loved you
Because you were like no other

You carried me whole
Through the storm
You strengthened my heart
With only the light of your soul
I liked and I loved you
Because you were poor
As I once was when I was a little girl.

My Heart Flutters By

Flutter my heart
With laughter and tears
Constricting a heartbeat
prolonging longevity

Flutter this heart
The life and its inequity
Embarking the soul's journey
Into antiquity preserving a dream

Flutter in heart
The depth of my pain
Lift now my thoughts
Always in the East a sun rises .

Flutter in air
Skip a heartbeat
 Smile at David
Passing a cloud and finding a star

Flutter into Infinity
Mystery in wings
away lethargy
Appear in magic and come away with me.

The Narcissist

I've been discarded
With a quick flicker by the hand
Like a cigarette spent in the ashtray of a world filled with insanity
Perhaps it's better
Than being thrown in the street
Like a prostitute owning her corner
Disregarded like a word on paper
But I like to think
I keep my wit upon me
Regardless of human atrocity
Pain exists only when you let it in
The cretin who's spent
On a night of uncertainty
Looking at pornography
Is lonelier than me
So I conceive
That perhaps it was the best thing that happened to me
Had I known the the sadist for the masochist
Believe me I would have changed everything.

Entitled

You're entitled to love
Somebody else
I know this to be true
Deep down inside
I want this for you

The happiness you gave me
Lingers inside my heart
I can't help feeling
A surrendering of my will

Pondering this difficulty
I relinquish my all
Inside whispers of adoration

I will always be there
As air moves
So does my heart make room
For I was the recipient of kindness
You were all encompassing gentleness

If you cannot love me
If you cannot love me
Then you must
Find the one that makes you happy
I will always have the pleasure
Of your most beautiful words

I will always have
the treasure of your name

Your book inspiring all my dreams
And mine your daily reveries

I will always keep you in my prayers
Inside the burning that
branded you to my heart

We will always be together
In finding you
I lived
I will always love you

Bear that in mind
For you and I bear each other's soul.

Muse

I once found a diamond
 I could not keep
It became obsolete
Glittered as it may have done
It carried the cross of my ardor
I threw it across the street
And the grass shone greener
Held by a purer nature
Glimmered in sunlit dew
And the blades so soft and true
Revealed the fragment of its shard
Reflected in the mirror of its bearer
In teardrops I can see much clearer
the wearer became its treasure
And the diamond was lost forever.

High

Today I am feeling majestic
Like the Phoenix rising from its ashes
Today I am feeling distinctive
As a Peacock's feather expanding
Today I feel gigantic
As Norse Viking's descendant
Today I am feeling eclectic
Like the sound of a hard drum beating
Today I am a soft tender hearted woman
A warrior on fire
All five foot two
Every inch is new
and brimming with desire
Beautifully adorned
With a Cameo pendant
Ready for all that's coming
Today I feel my strength
Powerful and bold
Earth trembling
Flower budding
Body shaking
Utterly female
Exhaling
Today I am soaring
The eagle beside mine
Piercing
Today I handle the stars
One by one
Today I explode
Inside the divine

With You
Inside the never ending twilight.

Turquoise

If I painted in the blue
I'd build you a brick house
Made of white clouds
Inviting you in to wander
Inside my turquoise bedding
Enveloped under a moss coverlet
I'd take you In a concert of
Abandonment
beautifully dreaming
In the Rose Woods
Where the mushrooms
Are accustomed wild and infinite.

Everlasting

Do you know where the skylark sings? Enchanting little thing, I happened upon him yesterday, capable of most anything, Black knight is fiend to Foe, though it is implied that no one works harder than the butterfly in tandem, the song of Life is all that she did carry, for all the world we hold in proverbial enchantment and seed Inside its best kept Knowledge, oh skylark when then Your nature sweet and true and call immediately a truce, the Earth a world of Heaven, Inside the softy moving flora of our so called companionship.

Daydream

Nothing happened You know
Though You wished for it all
Dreamed it all up into Your Life
You become what You have learned
And what you learned at will you let in

Nothing happened You know
It was like listening to a love song
I loved it more than you will ever know
As a friend I begged and I pleaded
The result was "not needed "

Nothing happened
That wasn't mine and your fault
It was destiny that called
That day
When you beckoned me back home
She laughed
at the irony of it all.

I Cannot Capture the Moon

I cannot capture the luminous moon
I cannot tell you the times I wished that I could
Cross her moonbeams immerse myself
In her white purity
Whiter than snow
Brighter than gold
I cannot tell you the lull of her voice
Her melody calls
Brings me to life
She renders me in mortal
A child on her carousel
She sways, she persuades
She keeps me awake
I cannot tell you how many times
I wished for someone at her portal
Under the gleam of her fairy light
She sends sparks across the Universe
I cannot capture the luminous moon
Only the wolf carries her cry
Under the covers of night
At the edge of her mountaintop.

The Sound's Calling

I listen to my heart
Because it's telling me to go forward
It wakes me up in the morning
And my mind follows it's query
I listen to it beat hard
Like a drum
Thump, thump
It is the sound
Of thunder and lightning
Crushing stones
like the waves crashing in the Ocean
I'm not afraid to get up in the morning
I know the day must get started
The call of the wild keeps on calling
My heartbeat keeps on going
Moving and flowing
Through the blood inside my veins
My ears hear it like rain
She keeps on falling
and I keep on moving
Hearing a song that keeps singing
I hear it and I keep going
I listen to my heart in the morning
And my mind follows her calling
She moves me
And My life is unfolding.

Unrequited Love

Life in her own way
Teaches her lesson

If you listen attentively
You can come to a clear cut Understanding
Don't get lost inside a dream
For the only way out
Is through your tears
I would have moved Heaven on Earth
For once ounce of pure blood
Yet fate did give to me
A taste of
unrequited love.

I cannot say
Why my stomach is fluttering
I am wondering
Does this feeling keep on coming
Downward spiraling
Glistening
What is happening
Something is moving
My heart is trembling
I feel a caress
A fragile kiss
And my mind
Goes wandering

Life teaches her lesson
Once I was lost in possession
Now I am simply

Swimming
In a vast ocean
Keeping my head above the waters.

Inspire

I was asked
On a particular night
To dream
Even more peculiar
To believe

I knew not how to perpetuate
This action in reality
Something called it familiarity
Perhaps even a filial legacy

Imagination
Is Energy in motion
But I don't have conclusive evidence
No proof of this simple pleasure
Taking place in a venture
Called dilly-dallying in action

Simply A-Day-dreaming
Of Periwinkle lions and stars with Silver lining
Under the Pomegranate lies Pegasus
The life giving Unicorn eating and submerged in discussion
What is fate and what of its repercussions?

Above the cloud forming elephants
Are strange mythical creatures
Call these faces, masks in high places
Of childish apparitions

Sleep induced pink cotton candy

Mirth and sweet merriment
With eyes wide open
Under blue sheets of silken wonder
The rainbow is a cover of Lavender
So often these fields appear
To my mind's eye
And the scent of loveliness awakens

What's in a dream?
Felicity and all that is contained within.
"Tonight I am a dream"

Emergent within the high womb of the Ocean
An elegant woman rises out of the wave of prostitution
She is the seat of evolution
The city of justice
The seed of repercussion

Dark hair flowing
Touching the ground
She is walking, glowing
Reaching with heart of devotion
A Place called Revolution

Inside her breast plate
Lives the steel of her forte
She rises and raises
The sword of admonition
Killing the soft sound of sullen apparitions

She swims in harmony
Inside the particles

Of a white cocoon
A Siren beneath the full moon
Thus becoming wind
Dust becoming her second skin

A creature is budding
Alive in the concrete
For even a tree sprouts from the lips
Of the mighty Deity

From a distance a voice calling a Gorgon ridiculous
The echo is a resounding tremor
History repeats in waves
the words a journey is never adjourned
Old Masters meeting with a new set of pupils
To form an encounter
Is there a price to pay for every conclusion?

A dreadful sea serpent
A Dragon coherent
The Griffin of pleasure
All come together
To serve the transparencies of spirit

Come friends let me ride
Upon the flames of knowledge
I will not burn
Inside the appetite of daemons
But harness the wings of a seraphim
Only the mighty queen can serve the heavens

Oh luminescent moon

Your crescent form
My swinging rope
I jump from crater to critter
Singing lullabies to puppet masters

Fantasy breathes inside my wings
Witness the spirit of beauty
in formed simplicity
Full bodied, tall standing
Strong and Erected
Wandering from birth to breath
Each child is at her breast
Is there a war formed inside her head?

The embodiment of Moray
Her fate called her
Nurturing the umbilical string of longevity
Whose soul impoverished
Amid a landmark of fertility?

With fluttering to and fro
The heart does beat a little bit more
Where is the flower that I adore
Where does the sun go when it is clouded

Does it dwell on a measure of hope?
What is the shelter of my thought?
Am I fallen without scope
Into the glass of wine port?

I am born a dreamer,
What privilege to bear a petal upon the shore
Friend to the pearl

Shell to iodine
Seaweed to stone
Water to Earth
Life and death
Fiend to foe
What joy
To walk barefoot upon the viridian lawn

Be it Moon or Universe
From East to West
She is home inside her nest
From coast to coast
From beast to animal
She sees clearly
Inside the mark of humanity

Her dream marking her birth
As sure as she breathes the fire of the Earth
She fades inside the madness
Of night calling her vicissitude
her right.

It's in the Little Things

I Found my love
In the middle of the Earth
Where the sun shone
He was made of gold

I lost my heart
To a young soul
Who keeps me whole
Found myself in the process of it all

In the abundance of a simple smile
He saw the intricacies of my life
What-more to be desired
To be understood, to desire
To be at his side

Of a sudden
In one single day
He struck with ardent flame
lightning and soul-filled trembling

He said,
It's in the glory of flowers and such little things
Those traveling ideas
Of simple pleasures, treasuries and garlands

That and the scent
Of dirt as you're planting
Awaiting the sprouting of summer
In a bud's rose filled coloring

And the water's great source of expansion
As it nourishes and evaporates into thin air
is a great expectation day!

These and those profound mysteries
When the sun blushes your skin
Tanned as the reptilian turtle
Called to the full moon
For future generation.

Of life when it is calling
That is complementary!
That is what completes me
Even temporarily.

Intrigued,
I believed in all things poetic
Isn't he my world's greatest poet?
Time has wings
I could only listen transfixed.

That is undoubtedly
the love of my life
I never doubted it once.

The love of my life
And this is what's nice
I've waited all my years
By chance, fortune smiled
My love is mine
And I his for all time.

I would have said
Anything to
keep you at my breast
As long as you'd rest
Inside my dwelling place
I would have met You
Anywhere on Earth
To lavish all my feeling
Celebrating joy and union
I would have been
A desperation in the making

Simply Mortal

Gone are the days
Of Zeus and Athena
Pegasus and Perseus
Oracles and Titans

All the remains
Are mortal skins
On an island forgotten

I can no longer
Ride my Pegasus
Astride
Bareback and wild

Man had stripped me naked
Of my pride
My riding crop fell to the ground
And fly higher than the beastly clouds

Into the arms of a butterfly
Into the heart of the city
Men still seeking a glory
That which no longer exists

Let the Gods cease and desist
In a dream Atlantis did speak.

Like a Pearl

My love is like a sheltered pearl
Unearthed

A womb unopened
Swaying in the oscillating
cradle of nurturing flesh

My love is in the color
Red

In the Iris of an oasis
She is the Atlantis

Swayingly Perplexed
My love is ardent and complex

Metamorphosing shell
She lives unperturbed upon the sand

My love returns to find me strewn upon the shore
She picks me up and takes me home

Cocooned inside the luminous moon
Harpooned by the Neptune

My love is the shimmering Mother of Pearl
The oyster of my living world.

My Skin is Pretty

My skin is pretty
I take good care of it

my skin is pretty
When I massage it

It's not just an outer shell of protection
It keeps me warm inside the elements

my shelter under the sun
My umbrella in the rain
I'm not cold, nor will I ever know
Burning from a source unknown

I'm not just a human being
I'm a glistening outer layer of proportionate endowment
like an egg in the foyer
I sit and embrace my armor

My skin is pretty
I wouldn't trade it
Not for one hair
On my entire body

When I look in the mirror
I smile
Because I think
That my skin is pretty
I am the wearer of such magnificent beauty.

And I open the door
Knowing I am unique person
Color, shape, scent and form.

I don't worry about those "needful things"

Because there is a vibratory pull toward me
She sings to me
And that is my entire world covering
Inside out of me.

I am Responsible

I share my thoughts
Like I would a glass of wine
Though I'm not one for preference
I do enjoy a good hard look
In the search for the ultimate answers
To ascertain a resolution
I ask the following questions:

Contemplate the difference between indifferent and making a difference
Finding a point of reference
It is perhaps undoubtedly one of the most violent periods in history
And we are living in it
We close an eye even both to the violence all around us

What is the stuff of today's humanity?

Vices, vices and so many transactions and non interactions
Bombs and violence
Go and shake hands
together as old time friends.

Today we are here
Today we are living
Tomorrow
Wine turns to blood
Glass shatters and
the Earth is obliterated.

The hand that once held it
Is now turned crimson

The fabric of our lives
Is living inside a brick house
Decorating it nicely to match
Art with decor
Who cares about the drugs sold to the poor?

Open your eyes
This is not living
Accept no more lies
Our children are the future
Deserving better
Than an irresponsible parent
Brainwashed by its own
by-product in the making
Simply called artificial insemination.

The Pine Tree

Fresh pine cones are born in the summer
When the air is crisp
And natural in its' progression
Each bee has her conquest
See how the resin drips down from its essence
Downward spiraling
Though in its capacity
It is never ambitious in falling
It is this source of excitement
That sticky combination
Is certainly confounding
A touch of inspiration
The stuff that binds
Portrays a form of completion
We never really think about it
The branches that hold
The needles that form it
The pine tree is a resilient adversary.

The Little Boat that Could

Well now I thought about
That little boat that could
With a tug, tug and a toot, toot
I thought about
So many little tunes
The oceans and the dunes
And the runes
And the Greco-Roman ruins
Stonehenge and the Druids
It came to me
That this voyage
Was ruined
By a little voice called
Time in opportune
The little boat that could
Became disillusioned
Incontro di sfortuna
(unfortunate meeting)
Never did much have a forte for dreaming
The web pulled everything back
As if a grand net
Into the grand scheme of things
Imagine the voyage
Imagine the emptiness
She aborted ship

No Hercules, neither Ulysses
No Iliad, no Odyssey
Just a plain girl recovering from tragedy
The little boat that could

Tugged at the heart
Tooted her very own horn
With a last call, taking her home
On the ferry of melancholy
She bids him Adieu.

What is the Price?

I am aware
My body is not for sale
My soul does not have a care
I brush the dust off my boots
Strange it was only yesterday
I fell off my rocking chair
The asteroid traveled
At super lightning speed
All the way down
To an exotic retreat
And here I am all freckle faced
Is there a sense in counting stars from space
When I carry blemishes on my skin
I think I may have counted too many
The night is dark
I close my eyes
Into the abyss of my life
Someone tell a joke
What more is there to provoke
I thought I saw a shooting star
Behave, beware she said
On the flight down from the sky
You've taken a piece of my heart

My Beloved

You set my soul on fire
How many minutes in the day
Lost in thoughts of you
Is it my fault?

The night is spent
Contemplating silence
Always this longing watching the hourglass
Wishing you could be near to me and hold me

As grains belong to the sand
I too want to hold your hand

Do you dream of me?
I try to pretend that it's a small matter
But the stars are witness
And the moon always listens

My beloved
Where are you now?
Filling your laughter
In someone else's earlobe

How long must I wait?
In the absence of thought
I'm lost

Tender is the night in waiting
I Know nothing
Except this infernal torment

Provoking in me a true haven
I know only the fire of Heaven

Oh Melancholy,
Should destiny in kindness unfold
Grant me one recourse
That I may live in sweet enchantment

Awakened into the night
For all its thunder light
Is contained in the murmurs
Of lovers' sighs

Awaken the night
For the stars burn
Breathing new life
In the ardent twilight

Open your eyes
A woman in love
Is a cove's paradise

I want to stay

I want to stay by your side

Until I Found You

Until I Found You
The Earth was a tiny little place
A dot in the Universe
I was the Tiny wave
That crested upon the shore

Until I Found You the tiny pearl
Called my heart
Was a hard difficult stone
Unpolished and worn
She barely shone

One day I found a shell
Laying upon the coverlet of sand
She whispered my name
She lured me away
She asked me to stay

My heart has never been the same
Until I found you

I could not see clearly

Nothing and everything
Can kept us apart

With every thought
I drank from the fountain of love

Desiring youth from the spring of life

Neptune came alive

Tumultuous waters became raptures
Of maritime components
The ugly duckling transformed the swan into an ocean of feathers

Holy is the dove in the springtime weather
For every master there is a servant

Nothing and all things can keep us together
Love smiled down in favor

Twas this fervent adoration
That led me to drink the water

from the fountain of revelation
I am forever a hungry nation

Now that I found you.

Desire

He had a well adjusted smile
From lips well rounded
Made to come alive
His teeth protruded
In elegance and not without brilliance
What wouldn't I have done
For one kiss
From his beautiful lips
If I think about it
Losing myself
inside his malleable gums
Wouldn't have hurt at all
He had a curious little smile
He was hungry for life
And not without a little embarrassment
He ate with ferociousness
I watched him
As I would a mother
Nursing from breast to milk to baby lips
I watched him
With desire in my eyes
I watched him nourish
His temple of God
I felt a rush to be at his side
I wanted to caress him with my loving eyes
I wanted his strokes at my breast
His arms at my side
He reached deep down inside
With his piercing grey eyes
Pulled out my heart

With my soul attached
And as pliable metal
Copper was welded with Iron
Placing fire within
Body to armor
At the head of a sedentary ship
Kiss to lips
He held me at the helm of
my burning desire...

www.ingramcontent.com/pod-product-compliance
Lightning Source LLC
Chambersburg PA
CBHW071540040426
42452CB00008B/1076